Shopping for Funeral Services

Federal Trade Commission | consumer.ftc.gov

Contents

When a loved one dies, grieving family members and friends often are confronted with dozens of decisions about the funeral — all of which must be made quickly.

What kind of funeral should it be?

What funeral provider should you use?

What are you legally required to buy?

Should you bury or cremate the body, or donate it to science?

What are the choices for a green funeral and burial?

What other arrangements should you plan?

How much is it all going to cost?

Each year, people grapple with these and many other questions as they spend billions of dollars arranging funerals for family members and friends.

Many funeral providers offer various "packages" of goods and services for different kinds of funerals. The Federal Trade Commission (FTC), the nation's consumer protection agency, wants you to know that when you arrange for a funeral, you have the right to buy goods and services separately. You do not have to accept a package that includes items you do not want.

Funeral Shopping Tips

Here are some tips to help you shop for funeral services:

- **Compare prices from at least two funeral homes.** Remember that you can supply your own casket or urn.

- **Ask for a price list.** The law requires funeral homes to give you written price lists for products and services.

- **Resist pressure to buy goods and services you don't really want or need.**

- **Avoid emotional overspending.** It's not necessary to have the fanciest casket or the most elaborate funeral to properly honor a loved one.

- **Recognize your rights.** Laws regarding funerals and burials vary from state to state. It's a smart move to know which goods or services the law requires you to purchase and which are optional.

- **Apply the same smart shopping techniques you use for other major purchases.** You can cut costs by limiting the viewing to one day or one hour before the funeral, and by dressing your loved one in a favorite outfit instead of costly burial clothing.

- **Shop in advance.** It allows you to comparison shop without time constraints, creates an opportunity for family discussion, and lifts some of the burden from your family.

The FTC Funeral Rule

The FTC enforces the Funeral Rule, which makes it possible for you to choose only the goods and services you want or need and pay only for those you select, whether you are making arrangements when a death occurs or pre-need. The Rule allows you to compare prices among funeral homes. The Rule does not apply to third-party sellers, such as casket or monument dealers, or to cemeteries that lack an on-site funeral home.

In brief, the Funeral Rule gives you the right to:

- **buy only the funeral goods and services you want.** You have the right to buy separate goods, like caskets, and separate services, like embalming or a memorial service. You don't have to accept a package with items you don't want.

- **get price information by telephone.** Funeral directors must give you price information on the telephone if you ask for it. You don't have to give them your name, address or telephone number first. Many funeral homes mail their price lists, although they aren't required to; some post them online.

- **get a written itemized price list when you visit a funeral home.** The funeral home must give you a General Price List (GPL) to keep. It must list 16 specific items and services, but it may include others, as well.

- **see a written price list for caskets before you see the actual caskets.** Sometimes, detailed casket price information is included on the funeral home's GPL. More often, though, it's provided on a separate casket price list. Get the price information before you see the caskets, so you can ask about lower-priced products that may not be on display.

- **see a written price list for outer burial containers.** Outer burial containers surround a casket in a grave. They are not required by any state law, but many cemeteries require them to prevent a grave from caving in. If the funeral home sells containers, but doesn't list the prices on the GPL, you have the right to look at a separate price list for containers before you see them. Look for a range of prices.

- **receive a written statement after you decide what you want, and before you pay.** It should show exactly what you are buying and the cost of each item. The funeral home must give you an itemized statement and the total cost immediately after you make the arrangements. The statement has to identify and describe any legal, cemetery or crematory requirements that require you to pay for any particular goods or services.

- **use an "alternative container" instead of a casket for cremation.** No state or local law requires the use of a casket for cremation. A funeral home that offers cremations must tell you that alternative containers are available, and must make them available. The containers might be made of unfinished wood, pressed wood, fiberboard or cardboard.

- **provide the funeral home with a casket or urn you purchase elsewhere.** The funeral provider cannot refuse to use a casket or urn you bought online, at a local store or somewhere else, and it can't charge you a fee to use it. The funeral home cannot require you to be on site when the casket or urn is delivered to them.

- **make funeral arrangements without embalming.** No state law requires routine embalming for every death. Some states require embalming or refrigeration if the body is not buried or cremated within a certain time; some states don't require those services at all. In most cases, refrigeration is an acceptable alternative. Services like direct cremation and immediate burial don't require any form of preservation. Many funeral homes have a policy requiring embalming if the body is to be publicly viewed, but this is not required by law in most states. Ask if the funeral home offers private family viewing without embalming. If some form of preservation is a practical necessity, ask the funeral home whether refrigeration is available.

Types of Funerals

Every family is different, and each wants its own type of funeral. Funeral practices are influenced by religious and cultural traditions, costs and personal preferences. These factors help determine whether the funeral will be elaborate or simple, public or private, religious or secular, and where it will be held. They also influence whether the body will be present at the funeral, if there will be a viewing or visitation, and if so, whether the casket will be open or closed, and whether the remains will be buried or cremated.

Full-service Funeral

This type of funeral, often referred to by funeral providers as a "traditional" funeral, usually includes a viewing or visitation and formal funeral service, use of a hearse to transport the body to the funeral site and cemetery, and burial, entombment, or cremation of the remains.

It is generally the most expensive type of funeral. In addition to the funeral home's basic services fee, costs often include embalming and dressing the body; rental of the funeral home for the viewing or service; and use of vehicles to transport the family if they don't use their own. The costs of a casket, cemetery plot or crypt, and other funeral goods and services are additional.

Immediate Burial

The body is buried shortly after death, usually in a simple container. No viewing or visitation is involved, so no embalming is necessary. A memorial service may be held at the graveside or later. Direct burial usually costs less than the "traditional" full-service funeral. Costs include the funeral home's basic services fee, as well as transportation and care of the body, the purchase of a casket or burial container and a cemetery plot or crypt. If the family chooses to be at the cemetery for the burial, the funeral home often charges an additional fee for a graveside service.

Direct Cremation

The body is cremated shortly after death, without embalming. The cremated remains are placed in an urn or other container. No viewing or visitation is involved. The remains can be kept in the home, buried, placed in a crypt or niche in a cemetery, or buried or scattered in a favorite spot. Direct cremation usually costs less than the "traditional" full-service funeral. Costs include the funeral home's basic services fee, as well as transportation and care of the body. A crematory fee may be included or added to the funeral home's fee. There also will be a charge for an urn or other container. The cost of a cemetery plot or crypt is added only if the remains are buried or entombed.

Funeral providers who offer direct cremations must make an alternative container available to use in place of a casket.

Choosing a Funeral Provider

In most states you don't have to use a funeral home to plan and conduct a funeral. However, some people find the services of a professional funeral home to be a comfort, because they have little experience with the details and legal requirements involved.

People often select a funeral home or cemetery because it's close to home, has served the family in the past, or has been recommended by someone they trust. But by limiting the search to just one funeral home, they may risk paying more than necessary for the funeral or narrowing their choice of goods and services.

Comparison Shopping

Comparison shopping may be easier if it's done before the need for a funeral arises. Thinking ahead can help you make informed and thoughtful decisions about funeral arrangements. It allows you to choose the specific items you want and need, and to compare the prices several funeral providers charge.

If you visit a funeral home in person, the funeral provider is required by law to give you a general price list (GPL) listing at least 16 specific items and services the home offers. If the GPL does not include specific prices of the caskets or outer burial containers the provider sells, the law requires the provider to show you the price lists for those items before showing you the items.

Sometimes it's more convenient and less stressful to "price shop" funeral homes by telephone. The Funeral Rule requires funeral directors to provide price information on the phone to any caller who asks for it. In addition, many funeral homes mail their price lists, although they aren't required to; some post them online.

When comparing prices, be sure to consider the total cost of all items, in addition to the costs of single items. Every funeral home should have price lists that include all the items essential for the different types of arrangements it offers. Many funeral homes offer package funerals that may cost less than buying individual items or services. Offering package funerals is permitted by law, as long as an itemized price list also is provided. But you can't accurately compare total costs unless you use the price lists.

There's a trend toward consolidation in the funeral home industry, and many neighborhood funeral homes may appear to be locally owned when in fact, they're owned by a national corporation. If this issue is important to you, you may want to ask if the funeral home is independent and locally owned.

Funeral Costs

Funeral costs include basic services fee for the funeral director and staff, charges for other services and merchandise, and cash advances. Make copies of the checklist at the middle of this booklet. Use it when you shop with several funeral homes to compare costs.

After you make arrangments, the funeral provider must give you an itemized statement of the total cost of the funeral goods and services you have selected. If you select a cash advance item, such as obituary notices, that the funeral provider will get from another business and the provider doesn't know the exact cost of the item yet, the provider must give you a written "good faith estimate" of the cost. This statement also must disclose any legal, cemetery or crematory requirements that require you to pay for any particular goods or services.

The Funeral Rule does not require any specific format for this information. Funeral providers may include it in any document they give you at the end of your discussion about funeral arrangements.

Basic Services Fee

The Funeral Rule allows funeral providers to charge all customers a basic services fee. The basic services fee includes services that are common to all funerals, regardless of the specific arrangement. These include funeral planning, securing the necessary permits and copies of death certificates, preparing the notices, sheltering the remains, and coordinating the arrangements with the cemetery, crematory or other third parties. The fee does not include charges for optional goods or services.

Other Goods and Services

Optional goods and services may include transporting the remains; embalming and other preparation; use of the funeral home for the viewing, ceremony or memorial service; use of equipment and staff for a graveside service; use of a hearse or limousine; a casket, outer burial container or alternate container; and cremation or interment.

Embalming

Many funeral homes require embalming if you're planning a viewing or visitation. But embalming generally is not necessary or legally required if the body is buried or cremated shortly after death. Eliminating this service can save you hundreds of dollars. Under the Funeral Rule, a funeral provider:

- may not provide embalming services without permission

- may not falsely state that embalming is required by law

- must disclose in writing that embalming is not required by law, except in certain special cases, such as a funeral with a viewing

- may not charge a fee for unauthorized embalming unless embalming is required by state law

- must disclose in writing that you usually have the right to choose a disposition, like direct cremation or immediate burial, that does not require embalming if you do not want embalming

- must disclose in writing that some funeral arrangements, such as a funeral with viewing, may make embalming a practical necessity and, if so, a required purchase

As far back as the ancient Egyptians, people have used oils, herbs and special body preparations to help preserve the bodies of their dead. Yet, no methods have been devised to preserve a body in the grave indefinitely. The Funeral Rule prohibits funeral providers from telling you that it can be done. For example, funeral providers may not claim that either embalming or a particular type of casket will preserve the body of the deceased for an unlimited time.

Caskets

For a "traditional" full-service funeral:

A casket often is the single most expensive item in a "traditional" full-service funeral. Caskets vary widely in style and price and are sold primarily for their visual appeal. Typically, they're constructed of metal, wood, fiberboard, fiberglass or plastic. Although an average casket costs slightly more than $2,000, some mahogany, bronze or copper caskets may sell for $10,000 or more.

When you visit a funeral home or showroom to shop for a casket, the Funeral Rule requires the funeral director to show you a list of caskets the company sells, with descriptions and prices, before showing you the caskets. Industry studies show that the average casket shopper buys one of the first three models shown, generally the middle-priced of the three.

So it's in the seller's best interest to start out by showing you higher-end models. If you haven't seen some of the lower-priced models on the price list, ask to see them — but don't be surprised if they're not prominently displayed, or not on display at all.

Funeral Pricing Checklist

Make copies of this page and check with several funeral homes to compare costs.

Funeral Goods & Services	Company A	Company B	Company C
Basic services of funeral director and staff			
Transfer body to funeral home			
Transfer body to another funeral home			
Receive body from another funeral home			
Direct cremation: funeral home charge			
Direct cremation: crematory charge			
For cremation: alternative container or rental casket			
Urn for cremated remains			
Immediate burial			
Embalming			
Other preparation of the body			
Casket			
Casket model number or description			

(product model number or description)			
Grave liner or vault			
Liner/vault model number or description			
Use of staff and facility:			
– for viewing or visitation			
– for funeral or memorial service			
Use of staff and equipment: for graveside service			
Hearse			
Limousine or other vehicles			
Subtotal			
Cemetery Goods & Services			
Cemetery plot, crypt or niche			
Endowment care fee			
Opening and closing plot, crypt or niche			
Marker or monument and set up fee			
Total			

Traditionally, caskets were sold only by funeral homes. But more and more, showrooms and websites operated by "third-party" dealers are selling caskets. You can buy a casket from one of these dealers and have it shipped directly to the funeral home. The Funeral Rule requires funeral homes to agree to use a casket you bought elsewhere, and doesn't allow them to charge you a fee for using it.

No matter where or when you're buying a casket, it's important to remember that its purpose is to provide a dignified way to move the body before burial or cremation. No casket, regardless of its qualities or cost, will preserve a body forever. Metal caskets frequently are described as "gasketed," "protective" or "sealer" caskets. These terms mean that the casket has a rubber gasket or some other feature that is designed to delay the penetration of water into the casket and prevent rust. The Funeral Rule forbids claims that these features help preserve the remains indefinitely because they don't. They just add to the cost of the casket.

Most metal caskets are made from rolled steel of varying gauges — the lower the gauge, the thicker the steel. Some metal caskets come with a warranty for longevity. Wooden caskets generally are not gasketed and don't have a warranty for longevity. They can be hardwood like mahogany, walnut, cherry or oak, or softwood like pine. Pine caskets are a less expensive option, but funeral homes rarely display them. Manufacturers of both wooden and metal caskets usually offer warranties for workmanship and materials.

For cremation:

Many families that choose cremation rent, rather than buy, a casket from the funeral home for the visitation and funeral. If you opt for visitation and cremation, ask about the rental option. For those who choose a direct cremation without a viewing or other ceremony with the body present, the funeral provider must offer an inexpensive unfinished wood box or alternative container, a non-metal enclosure — pressboard, cardboard or canvas — that is cremated with the body.

Under the Funeral Rule, funeral directors who offer direct cremations:

- may not tell you that state or local law requires a casket for direct cremations, because none do;

- must disclose in writing your right to buy an unfinished wood box or an alternative container for a direct cremation; and

- must make an unfinished wood box or other alternative container available for direct cremations.

Burial Vaults or Grave Liners

Burial vaults or grave liners, also known as outer burial containers, are commonly used to prevent the ground from caving in as a casket deteriorates over time. A grave liner is made of reinforced concrete and covers only the top and sides of the casket. A burial vault is more substantial and expensive than a grave liner. It surrounds the casket in concrete or another material and may be sold with a warranty of protective strength.

State laws do not require a vault or liner, and funeral providers may not tell you otherwise. However, keep in mind that many cemeteries require some type of outer burial container to prevent the grave from sinking in the future. Neither grave liners nor burial vaults are designed to prevent the eventual decomposition of human remains. It is illegal for funeral providers to claim that a vault will keep water, dirt, or other debris from penetrating into the casket if that's not true.

Before showing you any outer burial containers, a funeral provider is required to give you a list of prices and descriptions. It may be less expensive to buy an outer burial container from a third-party dealer than from a funeral home or cemetery. Compare prices from several sources before you select a model.

Cash Advances

Cash advances are fees charged by the funeral home for goods and services it buys from outside vendors on your behalf, including flowers, obituary notices, pallbearers, officiating clergy, and organists and soloists. Some funeral providers charge you their cost for the items they buy on your behalf. Others add a service fee to the cost. The Funeral Rule requires those who charge an extra fee to disclose that fact in writing, although it doesn't require them to specify the amount of their markup. The Rule also requires funeral providers to tell you if there are refunds, discounts, or rebates from the supplier on any cash advance item.

Cemetery Goods and Services

The FTC's Funeral Rule does not cover cemeteries and mausoleums unless they sell both funeral goods and funeral services.

When you buy a cemetery plot, cost is not the only consideration. The location of the cemetery and whether it meets the requirements of your family's religion are important, as well. Additional considerations include what, if any, restrictions the cemetery places on burial vaults purchased elsewhere, the type of monuments or memorials it allows, and whether flowers or other remembrances may be placed on graves.

Most cemeteries require you to purchase an outer burial container, which will cost several hundred dollars. There are charges — usually hundreds of dollars — to open a grave for interment and additional charges to fill it in. Perpetual care on a cemetery plot sometimes is included in the purchase price, but it's important to clarify that point before you buy the plot. If it's not included, look for a separate endowment care fee for maintenance and groundskeeping.

If you plan to bury cremated remains in a mausoleum or columbarium, you can expect to purchase a crypt, pay opening and closing fees, and pay for endowment care and other services.

Veterans Cemeteries

All military veterans are entitled to a free burial in a national cemetery and a grave marker. This eligibility extends to some civilians who provided military-related service and some Public Health Service personnel.

Veterans' spouses and dependent children also are entitled to a plot and marker in a national cemetery. There are no charges for opening or closing the grave, for a vault or liner, or for setting the marker in a national cemetery. The family generally is responsible for other expenses, including transportation to the cemetery. For more information, visit the Department of Veterans Affairs. To reach the regional Veterans Affairs office in your area, call 1-800-827-1000.

In addition, many states have established veterans cemeteries. Eligibility requirements and other details vary. Contact your state for more information.

You may see ads for so-called "veterans' specials" by commercial cemeteries. These cemeteries sometimes offer a free plot for the veteran, but charge exorbitant rates for an adjoining plot for the spouse, as well as high fees for opening and closing each grave. Evaluate the bottom-line cost to be sure the special is as special as you may be led to believe.

Pre-need Arrangements

An increasing number of people are designating their funeral preferences, planning their own funerals, and sometimes paying for them in advance. They see funeral planning as an extension of estate planning.

Thinking ahead can help you make informed and thoughtful decisions about the specific items you want and need. It also spares your survivors the stress of making these decisions. You can make arrangements directly with a funeral establishment.

When planning a funeral pre-need, consider where the remains will be buried, entombed, or scattered. In the short time between the death and burial of a loved one, many family members find themselves rushing to buy a cemetery plot or grave — often without time for careful thought or a personal visit to the site.

You may wish to make decisions about your arrangements in advance, but not pay for them in advance. Over time, businesses may close or change ownership. Prices may go up, or in some areas with increased competition, prices may go down. It's a good idea to review and revise your decisions every few years, and to make sure your family is aware of your wishes.

Put your preferences in writing, give copies to family members and your attorney, and keep a copy in a handy place. Don't designate your preferences in your will, because a will often is not found or read until after a funeral. Avoid putting the only copy of your preferences in a safe deposit box. That's because your family may have to make arrangements on a weekend or holiday, before the box can be opened.

Prepaying
Millions of Americans have entered into contracts to arrange their funerals and prepay some or all of the expenses involved. State law governs the prepayment for funeral goods and services; various states have laws to help ensure that advance payments are available to pay for funeral products and services when they're needed. But protections vary widely from state to state, and some state laws offer little or no effective protection. Some state laws require the funeral home or cemetery to place a percentage of the prepayment in a state-regulated trust or

to purchase a life insurance policy with the death benefits assigned to the funeral home or cemetery.

If you're thinking about prepaying for funeral goods and services, it's important to consider the answers to these questions:

- **What are you are paying for?** Are you buying only merchandise, like a casket and vault, or are you purchasing funeral services as well?

- **What happens to the money you paid?** States have different requirements for handling funds paid in advance for funeral services.

- **What happens to the interest income on money you pay?**

- **Are you protected if the firm you dealt with goes out of business?**

- **Can you cancel the contract and get a full refund if you change your mind about the items you bought or the arrangments you made?**

- **What happens if you move or die while away from home?**

Be sure to tell your family about the plans you made; let them know where the documents are filed. If your family isn't aware that you made plans, your wishes may not be carried out. And if family members don't know that you prepaid the funeral costs, they could end up paying for the arrangements too. You may wish to consult an attorney on the best way to ensure that your wishes are followed.

Funeral Terms

Here are terms you will encounter when planning a funeral.

Alternative container: An unfinished wood box or other non-metal receptacle without ornamentation, often made of fiberboard, pressed wood or composition material; it generally costs less than a casket.

Casket: A rigid container usually made of wood or metal, designed to hold remains.

Cemetery property: A grave, crypt, or niche in a cemetery.

Cemetery services: Opening and closing graves, crypts or niches; setting up grave liners, vaults or markers; maintaining cemetery grounds and facilities.

Columbarium: A room or building with niches that hold urns containing cremated remains.

Cremation: A heating process that incinerates human remains.

Crypt: A space in a mausoleum or other building that holds cremated or whole remains.

Direct cremation: Disposing of remains by cremation without having a formal viewing, visitation, or ceremony with the body present.

Disposing, disposition: Placing cremated or whole remains in their final resting place.

Endowment care: Maintaining a cemetery facility including grounds, plantings, roadways and water systems.

Endowment care fee: Money collected from cemetery property buyers and placed in trust to pay for cemetery maintenance.

Funeral ceremony: A service commemorating a deceased person with the body present.

Funeral provider: Any person, partnership or corporation that sells or offers to sell funeral goods and funeral services to the public.

Funeral services: Any services that care for and prepare bodies for burial, cremation or other final disposition and arrange, supervise or conduct a funeral ceremony or final disposition of remains.

Grave: A space in the ground for the burial of remains.

Grave liner: A type of outer burial container that covers the top and sides of a casket in a grave.

Graveside service: A service commemorating a deceased person held at a cemetery before burial.

Immediate burial: Disposing of remains by burial without having a formal viewing, visitation, or ceremony with the body present before the graveside service.

Interment: Placing remains in a grave, tomb or niche.

Inurnment: Placing cremated remains in an urn.

Marker: An inscribed stone that stands or is laid over a grave.

Mausoleum: A building in which remains are buried or entombed.

Memorial service: A ceremony commemorating a deceased person without the body present.

Niche: A space in a columbarium, mausoleum or wall to hold an urn.

Outer burial container: A structure that partially or completely surrounds a casket in a grave.

Urn: A container to hold cremated remains.

Vault: A type of outer burial container that surrounds a casket in a grave.

Contact Information

Most states have a licensing board that regulates the funeral industry. You may contact the board in your state for information or help. For more information about funeral arrangements and options, you can contact business, professional and consumer groups including:

AARP
Nonprofit organization that helps people 50 and older improve the quality of their lives.

601 E Street, NW
Washington, DC 20049
Toll-Free: 1-888-687-2277
www.aarp.org

Council of Better Business Bureaus
Private, nonprofit organization that promote ethical business standards and voluntary self-regulation of business practices.

3033 Wilson Blvd. Suite 600
Arlington, VA 22201
1-703-276-0100
www.bbb.org/us/

Cremation Association of North America

Association of crematories, cemeteries, and funeral homes that offer cremation.

499 Northgate Parkway
Wheeling, IL 60090-2646
1-312-245-1077
www.cremationassociation.org

Federal Trade Commission

Federal agency that enforces the funeral rule and works to prevent business practices that are anticompetitive, deceptive, or unfair to consumers.

600 Pennsylvania Avenue, NW
Washington, DC 20580
Toll-Free: 1-877-FTC-HELP
www.ftc.gov

Funeral Consumers Alliance

Nonprofit organization dedicated to protecting a consumer's right to choose a meaningful, dignified, affordable funeral.

33 Patchen Road
South Burlington, VT 05403
Toll-Free: 1-800-865-8300
www.funerals.org

Funeral Ethics Organization

Organization that promotes ethical dealings in all death-related transactions.

87 Upper Access Road
Hinesburg, VT 05461
1-802-482-6021
www.funeralethics.org

Green Burial Council

Nonprofit organization that encourages environmentally sustainable death care practices and helps consumers identify "green" cemetery, funeral, and cremation services.

1601 North Sepulveda, Suite 152
Manhattan Beach, CA 90266
Toll-Free: 1-888-966-3330
www.greenburialcouncil.org

International Cemetery, Cremation and Funeral Association

International trade association representing the cemetery, funeral service, cremation, and memorialization profession. It offers informal, free mediation of consumer complaints about cemetery services or policies.

107 Carpenter Drive, Suite 100
Sterling, VA 20164
Toll-Free: 1-800-645-7700
www.iccfa.com

Jewish Funeral Directors of America

International association of funeral homes serving the Jewish community.

107 Carpenter Drive, Suite 100
Sterling, VA 20164
Toll-Free: 1-888-477-5567
www.jfda.org

National Funeral Directors and Morticians Association

National association of primarily African-American funeral providers.

6290 Shannon Parkway
Union City, GA 30291
Toll free: 1-800-434-0958
www.nfdma.com

National Funeral Directors Association

Educational and professional association of funeral directors; provides consumer information and advice by telephone.

13625 Bishop's Drive
Brookfield, WI 53005
Toll-Free: 1-800-228-6332
www.nfda.org

Order of the Golden Rule

International association of independent, family-owned funeral homes.

3520 Executive Center Drive, Suite 300
Austin, TX 79731
Toll-Free: 1-800-637-8030
www.ogr.org

Selected Independent Funeral Homes

Association of independent locally-owned funeral homes.

500 Lake Cook Road, Suite 205
Deerfield, IL 60015
Toll-Free: 1-800-323-4219
www.selectedfuneralhomes.org

U.S. Department of Veterans Affairs

Federal agency that provides care and services to veterans and beneficiaries.

810 Vermont Avenue, NW
Washington DC 20420
Toll-Free: 1-800-827-1000
www.va.gov

U.S. Department of Veterans Affairs
National Cemetery Administration

Provides burial services in veteran's cemeteries for veterans and family members. Maintains cemeteries nationwide.

810 Vermont Avenue, NW
Washington DC 20420
Toll-Free: 1-800-827-1000
www.cem.va.gov

Solving Problems

If you have a problem concerning funeral matters, it's best to try to resolve it first with the funeral director. If you are dissatisfied with the funeral services you receive, the Funeral Consumers Alliance offers advice on how to resolve a problem. You also can contact your state or local consumer protection agencies. Check your telephone directory for phone numbers or visit www.naag.org for a list of state Attorneys General.

In addition, you can file a complaint with the FTC. The FTC works to prevent fraudulent, deceptive and unfair business practices in the marketplace and to provide information to help consumers spot, stop and avoid them. To file a complaint or get free information on consumer issues, visit consumer.ftc.gov or call toll-free, 1-877-FTC-HELP (1-877-382-4357); TTY: 1-866-653-4261.

Watch a video, *How to File a Complaint*, at consumer.ftc.gov/media to learn more. The FTC enters consumer complaints into the Consumer Sentinel Network, a secure online database and investigative tool used by hundreds of civil and criminal law enforcement agencies in the U.S. and abroad.

Federal Trade Commission
consumer.ftc.gov
September 2013

www.ingramcontent.com/pod-product-compliance
Lightning Source LLC
Chambersburg PA
CBHW081813170526
45167CB00008B/3417